Butterflies

Butterflies

by Edward S. Barnard

Reader's Digest

Published by The Reader's Digest Association, Inc.

London • New York • Sydney • Montreal

CONTENTS

Chapter 1

A butterfly grows up

It's summer and the Swallowtail butterfly flits round a meadow, delicately paddling the flowers as it searches for nectar to feed on. Soon it starts to lay tiny eggs on milk parsley or aromatic Mediterranean fennel.

The pale yellow egg cracks open in two weeks, and a tiny caterpillar crawls out and begins nibbling on a leaf. The caterpillar eats constantly, day and night. Every two or three days, it grows so big that the skin covering its body splits open, and a plumper caterpillar crawls out. Its green, black and orange markings help it to go unnoticed on leaves. To scare off birds, it can also produce some wobbly orange horns from its head that smell of ripe pineapple. Finally, after shedding its fourth skin, the caterpillar is about 5cm long and more than 3,000 times heavier than at its birth.

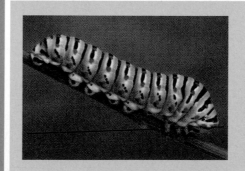

Plant food

The caterpillar at first feeds on milk parsley leaves, then moves up the stem to eat developing flower heads.

At last, the caterpillar has finished eating. It leaves the plant that it has fed on to find a protected spot where it can adopt a new disguise. Once it has found a place it likes, the caterpillar weaves a sticky button of silk on a stem and then, face up, makes a silk girdle around itself, so that it does not blow off in the wind. Shortly afterwards the caterpillar sheds its skin for the last time to reveal a beautiful brown or green vase-shaped case called a chrysalis (pronounced KRISS a liss).

Inside the case, it is silent. But incredible things are going on during this pupa stage. The caterpillar's body is changing into an adult butterfly. In about ten days, green-black wings are visible through the now see-through walls of the case. Finally the walls crack open, and a damp, crumpled butterfly crawls out.

For a few hours the Swallowtail butterfly clings to the case, resting. Fluids from its body flow into its wing veins. As the veins dry and harden, the wings become rigid, and it is able to fly away over the meadow.

Time to transform

After two weeks of munching leaves, a Swallowtail caterpillar glues the end of its body to the stem of a plant. Then it wriggles until its skin splits to reveal the chrysalis.

When its wings are dry and stronger, the Swallowtail flies away from its chrysalis.

chrysalis the case that covers and protects the caterpillar as its body is changing.

pupa another name for a chrysalis and also the name for this stage when the caterpillar's body is transformed into a butterfly.

As many as 250 million Monarch butterflies spend the winter in Mexico every year. Thousands of Monarchs perch on a single fir tree!

DID YOU KNOW?

Beautiful Monarch butterflies are sometimes seen in the UK but they come here by mistake. Every autumn, millions of them fly south from North America. Some get blown off course and arrive in the UK or on the Continent after crossing the Atlantic Ocean!

Swallowtails spend a lot of time feeding and moving from one meadow to another, darting, swooping and flashing their wings in the sunshine to attract suitable mates. After courtship, the female will aim to lay her eggs in a new meadow where there will be less competition from other Swallowtails and their caterpillars.

Swallowtail butterflies don't roam far, unlike other species, such as Red Admirals, Painted Ladies and Camberwell Beauties which can cover hundreds of miles.

The remarkable Monarch butterfly lives for up to six months and can travel thousands of miles. From North America, it heads south to Mexico, guided perhaps by the position of the sun. On windy days, it may fly as fast as 70 miles an hour: if it is very stormy, these butterflies can be carried eastwards – right across the Atlantic Ocean!

Bad taste here

Monarch caterpillars feed on milkweed plants and absorb their poison. This gives the adult butterfly a nasty taste that keeps away predators.

Chapter 2

A butterfly's body

A butterfly has four wings –
two forewings and two
hindwings. The wing
markings are different for
each kind of butterfly.

Three in one

Butterflies, like grasshoppers and ants, are insects. Like all other insects, their bodies are divided into three parts – the head, thorax and abdomen.

● Many of a butterfly's sense organs are located in its head, including its eyes, two antennae for touching and smelling, and a mouthpart for drinking that is a long, narrow, flexible tube called a proboscis (pronounced pro BOS iss). Inside the head is the butterfly's brain.

● Behind the butterfly's head is its thorax. It is the anchor point for the butterfly's two pairs of wings and for its three pairs of legs. The legs have tasting and smelling sensors on their ends! Inside the thorax are muscles for the wings and legs and for the butterfly's heart, which pumps blood around the muscles and organs.

● Behind a butterfly's thorax is the abdomen. It contains a series of tubes that circulates air throughout the body. It also contains organs for reproduction and digestion.

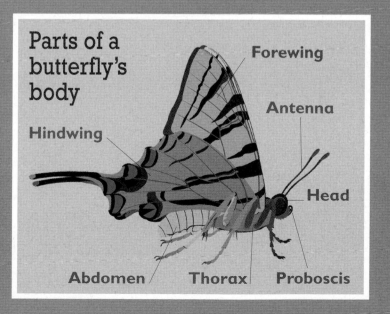

Parts of a butterfly's body

Forewing

Antenna

Hindwing

Head

Abdomen   Thorax   Proboscis

Butterfly or moth?

Butterflies and moths are the only insects with scales on their wings. Scales are what give the wings their colour. Butterflies and moths look a lot alike, but there are differences that will help you to tell them apart.

● Butterfly antennae have little knobs on their ends or their ends are slightly thickened. Moth antennae never have knobs, and they are different shapes, too.

● The bodies of butterflies are thinner than moth bodies.

● Most butterflies fly during the day. Most moths fly at night.

● Butterflies often rest with their wings held straight up. Moths usually spread their wings flat.

● Butterflies have less body hair than moths.

● Butterflies have brighter colours than moths, but there are plenty of exceptions. Some butterflies have dull colours, and some moths have beautiful colours.

Telltale antennae

Butterflies and moths use their antennae to smell, which helps them to find food and mates. Moths are active at night, when it is harder to see, so their antennae are often larger and more sensitive.

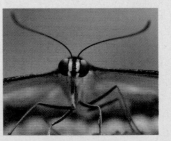

Butterfly

Moth

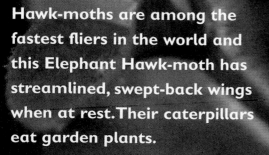
Hawk-moths are among the fastest fliers in the world and this Elephant Hawk-moth has streamlined, swept-back wings when at rest. Their caterpillars eat garden plants.

When a butterfly isn't feeding, it keeps its proboscis coiled like a garden hose.

Straw sipper

Unlike a caterpillar, a butterfly can't chew leaves. It can only sip liquids, such as flower nectar, tree sap and juice from fruit. It uses its mouthpart (the proboscis) like a straw, poking deep into flowers and sucking up their sugary nectar. The proboscis is very long, sometimes longer than the butterfly's body!

Eye contact

A butterfly's eyes are made up of thousands of tiny separate eyes. A butterfly sees in all directions and detects movements very well. It can see things close up well, but distant objects appear blurry. However, it sees ultraviolet light waves that we can't see – an ability that may help long-distance butterfly travellers, such as Monarchs, to navigate.

Flower food

Butterflies need lots of liquid and may visit hundreds of flowers in a day. They identify flowers by colour and seem to favour red ones.

Wings of beauty

Scientists group butterflies and moths into a category called Lepidoptera (pronounced leh puh DOP tuh ruh). Lepidos is a Greek word meaning 'scales'. Ptera is a Greek word meaning 'wings'.

The most beautiful parts of a butterfly are its two pairs of wings. The forewings, located closest to the head, are often larger than the hindwings. The tops and bottoms of the wings usually have different patterns and colours.

The wings of butterflies and moths are covered with millions of the tiny scales, which give them their distinctive colours. The powder on your fingers after you touch a butterfly's or moth's wings is actually thousands of these scales!

When a butterfly first emerges from its chrysalis, the veins in its wings are soft. After the butterfly pumps liquid into them, they harden. The veins help to make the wings rigid so that the butterfly can fly.

Colourful scales

The bright irridescent colours of butterfly wings are a physical effect due to sunlight breaking up on the wavy surface of the scales.

The Large Blue butterfly's wings are made up of a variety of colours that create a pattern which enables it to blend in as it flies among meadow flowers.

Chapter 3

Feeding
and flying

The Hickory Horned Devil, the caterpillar of the Royal Walnut moth, looks quite ferocious. But the 15cm caterpillar is perfectly harmless.

Eating machines

Butterflies and moths develop in four stages: egg, caterpillar, pupa and adult. The caterpillar is the feeding stage – a creature designed to eat and grow. All a caterpillar does, in fact, is eat and eat.

As the caterpillar eats, the cells in its body don't multiply, they simply inflate like balloons. Eventually the caterpillar's body swells up so much that its skin gets too tight and splits. The caterpillar then wriggles free of its old skin. This process occurs about four or five times in a caterpillar's life. Each time, the caterpillar nearly doubles in size.

Caterpillars have so many predators, such as birds and other insects, that their numbers don't build up enough to cause serious damage to the environment. Sometimes, though, there aren't enough predators to control caterpillar populations. Then they multiply so fast that they eat themselves out of house and home. Gypsy moth caterpillars, for example, sometimes chew up so many leaves in southern Europe that hundreds of acres are completely stripped.

Phoney feet offer a leg up

All caterpillars share a basic body design. The head has compound eyes, two tiny antennae and chewing mouthparts. The body is made up of 13 parts. The first three parts form the thorax, and each part has a pair of legs. The ten remaining parts form the abdomen. Five of those parts have a pair of false legs, called prolegs. The prolegs help the caterpillar move and grip twigs and leaves.

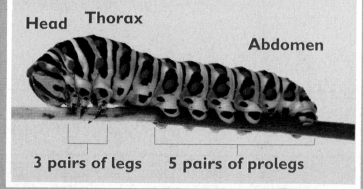

Head   Thorax   Abdomen

3 pairs of legs   5 pairs of prolegs

Flying tales

If a caterpillar is an eating machine, a butterfly is a flying machine. A butterfly's first defence against predators is to fly away from them. If you have ever tried to catch one, you know how easily it can flutter just out of reach.

Bad-tasting butterflies usually fly slower than butterflies that taste delicious. That's because predators don't chase them so they don't need speed to escape.

Bright, distinctive colours help to protect the Red Admiral butterfly, which is widespread in mainland Europe and also migrates and breeds in summer in the UK. It is black and white (warning colours in the animal kingdom) with red, which keeps away bird predators who learn to associate this colour scheme with a bad taste. The Red Admiral's dark underside helps to conceal it when it is resting.

Red Admirals love sunshine and flowers. When they fly, their brightly coloured wings ward off birds. When they are at rest with their wings folded, their dark underside helps them to blend into their surroundings.

Surviving
in the wild

Chapter 4

Caterpillar tricks

The Maple Spanworm caterpillar is the colour of tree bark. It can stretch out its body to look exactly like a twig!

This caterpillar has curled most of its upper body against its abdomen to create a big false head with two huge 'eyes'. A bent, pointed tail-end adds to the scary effect!

Caterpillars would seem to be easy targets for predators. They feed out in the open and they are slow moving. But caterpillars have ways of tricking other animals that are looking for a meal.

Some caterpillars have nasty poisonous spines and prickly hairs that make swallowing them very unpleasant! Others scrunch themselves into threatening positions when they are in danger so that they look much bigger than they really are. A few disguise themselves as bird droppings or other unappealing things. And some just look so fierce and dangerous that they scare off predators.

Several caterpillars build structures to protect themselves from predators. Some moth caterpillars, for example, spin silk tents in which they rest when they are not feeding. Certain Skipper butterfly caterpillars cover themselves with leaf tents.

Butterfly disguises

Unlike caterpillars, butterflies can escape from most predators by flying away. However, flying won't work as a defence against birds and bats because they can chase butterflies in the air. So some butterflies have colours and patterns that make them almost invisible when they are resting on tree trunks or perched among leaves.

Warning colours

Instead of blending into their environment, many butterflies do just the opposite. They stand out with bold colours and patterns that warn predators off. Some of these colourful butterflies, such as the orange-and-black American Monarchs are poisonous, and so predators definitely stay away. But several non-poisonous butterflies also use warning colours, tricking predators into looking elsewhere for a meal.

Eyes that scare

When it opens its wings suddenly, a butterfly with eye spots can often startle a predator long enough to escape.

Hanging off a leaf, a resting Brimstone butterfly manages to look exactly like another leaf, complete with veins and a brown stem.

Dead leaf?

Snout butterflies look like dead leaves with stems. When they fly in groups in early autumn, they resemble dry, fallen leaves blowing in the wind.

Chapter 5

Butterflies in the world

The Peacock butterfly, a common butterfly of Europe and Asia, lives farther north than it once did because of climate warming.

All kinds of butterflies

There are about 15,000 different kinds of butterflies in the world. They live on every continent except Antarctica.

Tropical rainforests are home to the greatest variety of butterflies. The world's largest and rarest butterfly, the Queen Alexandra's Birdwing, has a wingspan of up to 30cm! It lives in the rainforests of Papua New Guinea, which is north of Australia. Butterflies also live in the deserts, mountains and Arctic tundra.

The world's smallest butterfly, the Sinai baton blue, lives in the deserts of Egypt's Sinai Peninsula. It has a wingspan no wider than a thumbnail. The Apollo butterfly of the Himalayan Mountains lives only at altitudes of 5,000 metres or more above sea level!

Big and bad tasting

The world's biggest butterflies, the Birdwings of Southeast Asia, are bad tasting and poisonous. A predator only tries eating one once.

A global butterfly

Some kinds of butterflies live only in the wild where the plants they sip from grow. The Painted Lady butterfly isn't so picky. It eats from many different plants, and thus can live in many different places — in the wild and in city and farm environments.

The Painted Lady is extremely widespread and can be found on all continents except Antarctica and Australia. It spends the winter in warm places where temperatures stay above freezing. Then in spring, some Painted Ladies fly to places where they could not have survived in winter.

Colours that change

A Painted Lady's wings are black, brown, orange and white when opened, but grey, tan, black, white and pink when closed.

Perched on an orange slice, a Painted Lady butterfly sips juice with its long, skinny mouthpart, called a proboscis, that sucks up liquid like a straw.

The future of butterflies

Many kinds of butterflies are endangered. They are losing their habitats as land is cleared for farms and houses. Their numbers drop quickly when the wild plants that they lay their eggs on and eat from become scarce. One of the best ways to help butterflies is to join an organisation working to protect the natural habitats in which these beautiful and amazing insects live.

Plant a butterfly garden

Even if your garden is small, you can still plant flowers that will lure butterflies. They like all sorts of brightly coloured flowers, especially buddleja, verbena and honeysuckle. Butterflies love overripe fruit, too.

FAST FACTS ABOUT BUTTERFLIES

SCIENTIFIC NAME	Swallowtail	*Papilio machaon*
	Painted Lady	*Vanessa cardui*
ORDER	Swallowtail	Lepidoptera
	Painted Lady	Lepidoptera
FAMILY	Swallowtail	Papilionidae
	Painted Lady	Nymphalidae
SIZE	Swallowtail	up to 9.5cm wide
	Painted Lady	up to 4.3cm wide
LIFE SPAN	Swallowtail	about 3-4 weeks
	Painted Lady	about 2 weeks
HABITAT	Swallowtail	meadows, hamlets, wetlands
	Painted Lady	fields, gardens, seashore

Some kinds of blue
butterflies are endangered.
One kind is now extinct. It
disappeared when its sand
dune habitat was turned
into a housing development.

GLOSSARY OF WILD WORDS

abdomen   the rear part of an insect's body that takes care of breathing, digesting and reproducing

antennae   a pair of organs on an insect's head for smelling and touching

caterpillar   the wormlike stage of a butterfly's development

chrysalis   a case that covers and protects a butterfly as it develops

endangered   a species of animal or plant in danger of extinction

forewings   the first pair of wings on a butterfly's thorax

gland   an organ that releases substances such as silk strands for attaching a chrysalis to a leaf

habitat   the natural environment where an animal or a plant lives

nectar   a sweet liquid made by flowers

migrate   to go from one place to another at certain times of the year to find food or to mate and give birth

wildWORD

metamorphosis when something changes shape dramatically, such as when a butterfly caterpillar transforms itself to a resting stage and then into an adult butterfly.

predator	an animal that hunts and eats other animals to survive		thorax	part of an insect's body located behind the head. Four wings and six legs are attached to it
proboscis	a butterfly's long, skinny mouthpart that works like a straw for sipping liquids		tundra	an area without trees in an Arctic region or on a high mountain with short plants and a frozen layer of soil underground
prolegs	stubby leg-like structures on the abdomens of caterpillars			
pupa	the resting stage in a butterfly's life during which it changes from a caterpillar to an adult		ultraviolet	light waves that cannot be seen by human beings
species	a group of plants or animals that are the same in many ways		warning colours	markings and bright colours on an animal that warn off predators

INDEX

CREDITS

Butterflies is an **All About Animals** fact book
Written by Edward S. Barnard

Published in 2010 in the United Kingdom by Vivat Direct Limited (t/a Reader's Digest),
157 Edgware Road, London W2 2HR

Editor: Rachel Warren Chadd
Designer: Nicola Liddiard
Art editor: Simon Webb

Reprinted in 2011

Adapted from *Butterflies* published by Reader's Digest Young Families Inc. in 2006.

Printing and binding Arvato Iberia, Portugal

ISBN: 978 0 276 44609 2
Book code: 640-018 UP0000-2
Oracle code: 504500016H.00.24